Life around the World
Clothes in Many Cultures

by Heather Adamson

Consulting Editor: Gail Saunders-Smith, PhD

Capstone press®

Mankato, Minnesota

Pebble Plus is published by Capstone Press,
151 Good Counsel Drive, P.O. Box 669, Mankato, Minnesota 56002.
www.capstonepress.com

1 2 3 4 5 6 12 11 10 09 08 07

Library of Congress Cataloging-in-Publication Data
Adamson, Heather, 1974–
    Clothes in many cultures / by Heather Adamson.
    p. cm.— (Pebble plus. Life around the world)
    Summary: "Simple text and photographs present clothing from many cultures"—Provided by publisher.
    Includes bibliographical references and index.
    ISBN-13: 978-1-4296-0018-7 (hardcover)
    ISBN-10: 1-4296-0018-7 (hardcover)
    1. Clothing and dress—Cross-cultural studies—Juvenile literature. I. Title. II. Series.
GT518.A33 2008
391—dc22   2006101947

Editorial Credits
Sarah L. Schuette, editor; Alison Thiele, set designer; Kara Birr, photo researcher

Photo Credits
Corbis/Reuters/Paul Mathews, 13
Peter Arnold Inc./Achim Pohl, 5; Michael Sewell, 7
Shutterstock/Bruce C. Murray, cover (Hawaii); Dario Diament, 1 (India); Elena Elisseeva, 21;
    Geir Olav Lyngfjell, 9; J.T. Lewis, 19; Lincoln Rogers, 17
SuperStock Inc./Baldev Kapoor, 15; Ray Laskowitz, 11

Note to Parents and Teachers

The Life around the World set supports national social studies standards related to
culture and geography. This book describes and illustrates clothes in many cultures. The
images support early readers in understanding the text. The repetition of words and
phrases helps early readers learn new words. This book also introduces early readers
to subject-specific vocabulary words, which are defined in the Glossary section. Early
readers may need assistance to read some words and to use the Table of Contents,
Glossary, Read More, Internet Sites, and Index sections of the book.

Table of Contents

Clothes to Wear

Around the world,
everyone wears clothes
for work or play.

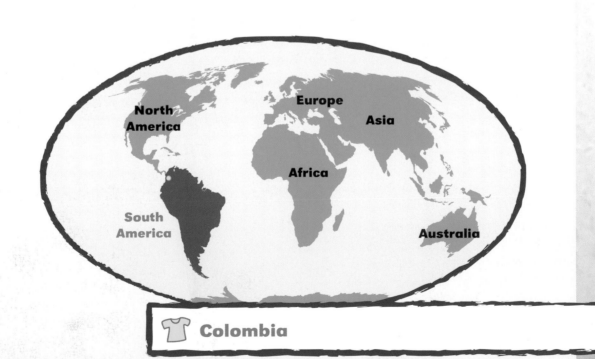

Colombia

Parkas keep people warm
on cold days.

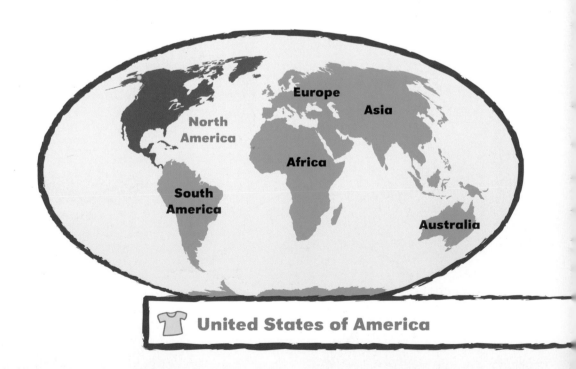

United States of America

Sarongs keep people cool
on hot days.

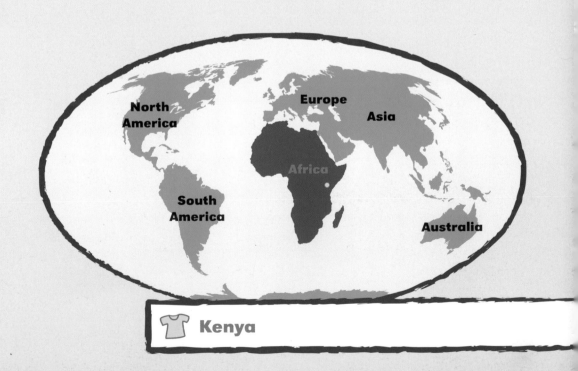

Kenya

Work Clothes

Office workers wear business suits to their jobs.

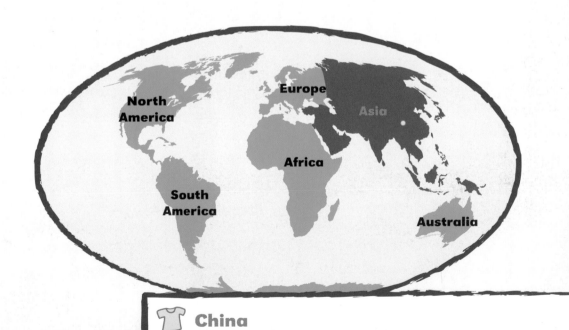

North America

Europe

Asia

Africa

South America

Australia

👕 China

Ranchers wear sturdy jeans
when they work outside.

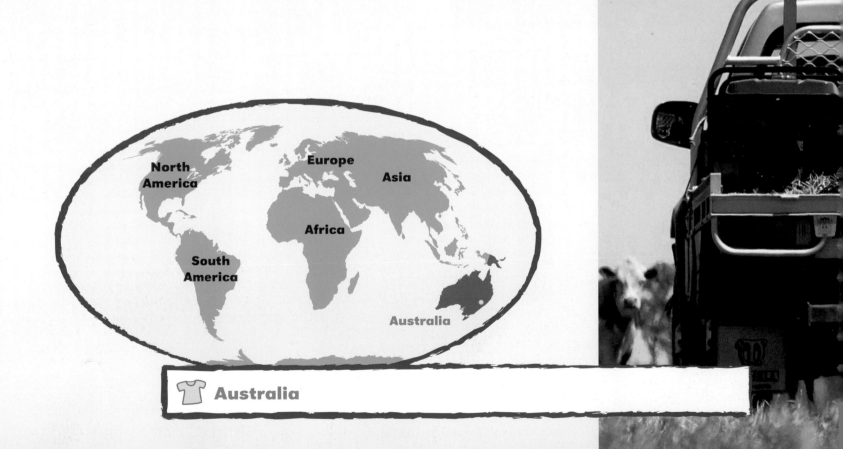

North America

Europe

Asia

Africa

South America

Australia

👕 Australia

Traditional Clothes

Brides and grooms wear
fancy clothes
on their wedding day.

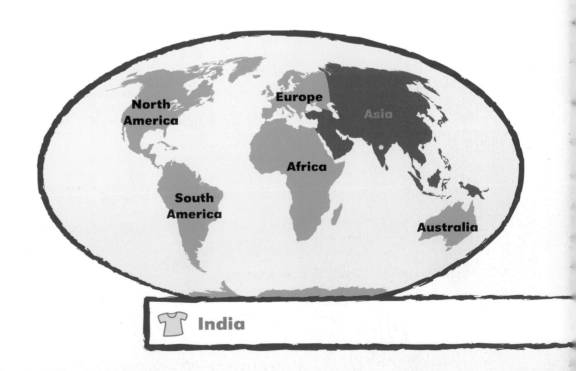

India

American Indians wear
bright colors to dance
at powwows.

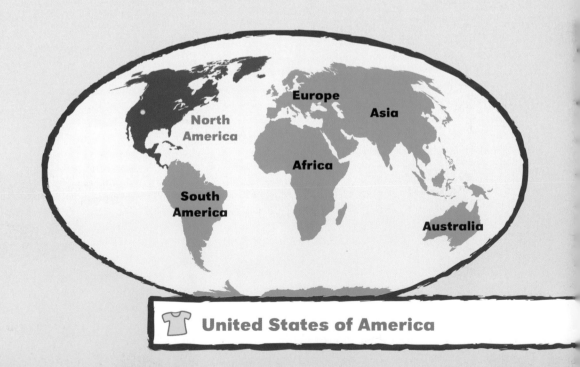

North America

Europe

Asia

Africa

South America

Australia

👕 **United States of America**

Scottish men wear
kilts in parades
and at ceremonies.

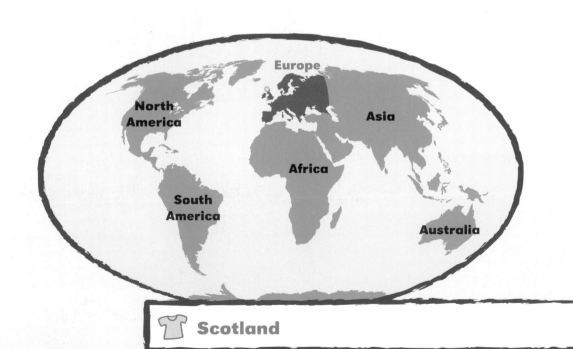

North
America

Europe

Asia

Africa

South
America

Australia

Scotland

Your Clothes

Clothes are different
around the world.
What did you wear today?

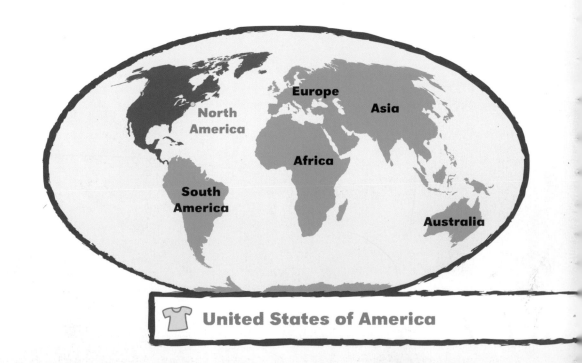

United States of America

Glossary

bride—a woman who is about to get married

business suit—a set of matching clothes that includes a jacket and pants or a jacket and skirt

ceremony—formal actions, words, and music performed to mark an important occasion

groom—a man who is about to get married

kilt—a plaid skirt with pleats or folds

parka—a large heavy coat made with fur

powwow—a social gathering where American Indians dance, tell stories, and celebrate traditions

sarong—a piece of cloth wrapped around the body

sturdy—strong and firm; jeans are sturdy and do not rip or tear easily.

Read More

Doudna, Kelly. *Clothing around the World.* Around the World. Edina, Minn.: Abdo, 2004.

Easterling, Lisa. *Clothing.* Our Global Community. Chicago: Heinemann, 2007.

Johansen, Heidi Leigh. *My Clothes.* Getting to Know My World. New York: PowerKids Press, 2005.

Internet Sites

FactHound offers a safe, fun way to find Internet sites related to this book. All of the sites on FactHound have been researched by our staff.

Here's how:

1. Visit *www.facthound.com*

2. Choose your grade level.

3. Type in this book ID **1429600187** for age-appropriate sites. You may also browse subjects by clicking on letters, or by clicking on pictures and words.

4. Click on the **Fetch It** button.

FactHound will fetch the best sites for you!

Index

Word Count: 79
Grade: 1
Early-Intervention Level: 12